I Feel Sick!

Mick Manning
and Brita Granström

FRANKLIN WATTS
LONDON•SYDNEY

To Louis Pasteur

First published in 2002
by Franklin Watts,
96 Leonard Street,
London EC2A 4XD

Franklin Watts Australia
45-51 Huntley Street
Alexandria
NSW 2015

The illustrations in this book
have been drawn by Brita

Text and illustrations © 2002 Mick Manning
and Brita Granström
Series editor: Rachel Cooke
Art director: Jonathan Hair

Printed in Hong Kong, China
A CIP catalogue record is available from
the British Library.
Dewey Classification 613
ISBN 0 7496 4299 8 (hbk)
ISBN 0 7496 4788 4 (pbk)

Contents

Catching a cold

I'm Tessa. I've got a runny nose, and I've been whispering and giggling with my friend all through class. Now I feel sick . . .

Illnesses like coughs, colds and flu are caused by germs. Germs spread by close contact - coughing, breathing, sneezing, all spread germs.

Passing it on!

I'm Abi, Tessa's friend.
I feel poorly, too.
Mum's kept me off
school today.

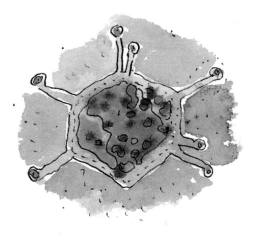

Germs are tiny living things, too
small to see just using our eyes.
A flu germ looks like this
through a microscope.

Germs like warm places to live
in - like people's bodies!

I'm Maggie, Abi's mum.
I've caught the bug now!
Flu always gives me
an upset tummy.
Thank goodness Abi's
dad is coming home . . .

*Germs can affect people in
different ways.*

*Always wash your hands
after going to the loo.
You'll wash off any germs
as well as dirt.*

11

Coughs and sneezes

I'm Mo, Abi's dad.
I'm glad I left work early -
I'm all stuffed up!
Aahhhahhchooo!

Germs can spread easily by coughing and sneezing. Put your hand to your mouth when you cough, or sneeze into a hanky to help stop germs spreading.

I'm Dave - the taxi driver. I can't manage my tea. I feel really dodgy! I'm always catching stuff off my customers.

Your body fights diseases best if you have a healthy diet, not just lots of junk food and sweets.

Eat plenty of fresh fruit and vegetables – the vitamins they contain, particularly vitamin C, can protect you against colds.

Stay in bed

I'm Mary, Dave's wife. I feel terrible! I know I shouldn't be up but we've no milk or anything . . .

If you do get sick, you need to rest. This lets your body concentrate on making you better.

I'm Misha. I run the shop. I feel hot and dizzy and I can't stop coughing!

Sometimes, you have a temperature when your body is trying to fight off germs.

18

At the doctor's

I'm Conner.
I feel like rubbish . . .
I don't know where I
caught this bug. Now
I've got to see the doctor.

You can pick up germs just about
anywhere, particularly indoors: in
shops, in buses, in the classroom
– even in doctors' waiting rooms.

It's me, Tessa, again. Mum's getting me some medicine. The doctor said it will help keep my temperature down. I hope it tastes nice!

Sometimes when we are sick, medicine will help us feel better.

Medicines and tablets are not sweets and can be dangerous. NEVER take them unless a grown-up gives them to you.

The best medicine

Abi here. The doctor says the best medicine for me is bed, lots to drink and lots of fresh fruit.

Although doctors do give you medicine when a cold turns nasty – they often prefer to let your body heal itself.

You need to drink lots of water when you've got a cold.

Germ ideas

Find out more about germs, feeling sick and, most importantly, staying healthy.

The history of a cold

If you or someone you know catches a cold, work out where it came from and who else caught it. Make a diagram to show the cold's history.

Watch it grow

Germs are everywhere - and they are not all bad! We use a type of germ to make cheese and yogurt.

Stir a teaspoon of natural yogurt into a cup of milk and leave in a warm place for a day or two. The germs in it will make more yogurt! Don't eat it, though. Some nasty germs may get in, too.

Design a poster

Eating fresh fruit and vegetables helps us to fight off colds. Make a poster telling everyone to eat more of them!

Be safe!

Remember, never take medicine or pills unless a grown-up says you can.

Germ words and index

cold A cold is a disease that lots of people get. It makes our nose snotty and our throat sore. Colds are caused by germs passing from person to person. Pages 6, 7, 14, 25

cough We cough when our throat is tickly or our lungs are full of gunge, making it hard to breathe. This often happens when we have a cold. Pages 7, 12, 13, 18

diet The food we eat. Page 14

flu Flu is a disease caused by germs and is easily passed from person to person. Flu tends to make our bodies achy and we run a temperature. Pages 7, 8, 9, 10

germs Tiny living things that are so small you can only see them with a microscope. Some germs cause diseases but others help us stay healthy. Pages 7, 8, 10, 13, 18, 20, 27

medicine Something we take when we are ill to make us better. Never take medicine unless an adult gives it to you. Pages 22, 25

sneeze We sneeze when air suddenly rushes out of our nose because it is tickly or we have a cold. Pages 7, 12, 13

temperature We say we have a temperature when our body gets hotter than it normally is. Pages 18, 22

upset tummy When we have an upset tummy, we have to go the toilet a lot and our poo is very runny. Page 10

vitamins Parts of our food that we need to be healthy. For example, vitamin C helps us fight off germs. Page 14